EDIE HARPER
COLORING BOOK

Edie Harper (1922–2010) is best known as a painter, photographer, and illustrator, although she also created jewelry, enamels, sculpture, silkscreen prints, and weavings. Harper expressed her sense of humor through her artworks, and the titles she gave them sometimes poked fun at her subjects. She also was very good at reducing images to their essential forms; her paintings often are made up of simple geometrical shapes, including rectangles, lines of different weight, triangles, circles, and crescents. Harper loved cats and, as you will see, she made many paintings of them, but she applied her playful, simplified style to other subjects as well.

We've selected twenty of Edie Harper's paintings for this coloring book; they are printed on the inside front and back covers so you can see her original color schemes. You might want to imitate Harper's colors or you might choose entirely different ones. The last three pages of the book are blank so you can draw and color your own pictures. Maybe you can use geometrical shapes to create portraits of your own favorite pets.

Pomegranate Kids
AGES 3 to 103!

All works of art were created by Edie Harper (American, 1922–2010).

1. Penny Candy
2. Spring Creeper
3. Summer Watch
4. Crazy Cat, Crazy Quilt
5. Noazark
6. Fishful Thinking
7. Cat in a Hatbox
8. Treehouse
9. Milking Megan the Moo Cow
10. Baskit
11. Winter Watch
12. Specially for You
13. Copy Cats
14. Orange Cat
15. Couch Petatoes
16. Tea with Penelope the Bee
17. Peepkin
18. Nine Tails
19. Kitten 'n Knittin'
20. Sleepy Time Tom

Pomegranate Communications, Inc.
Box 808022, Petaluma CA 94975
800 227 1428   www.pomegranate.com

Color illustrations © 2012 Estate of Edie Harper
Line drawings © Pomegranate Communications, Inc.
Catalog No. CB146
Designed and rendered by Susan Koop
Printed in Korea
21 20 19 18 17 16 15 14 13 12   10 9 8 7 6 5 4 3 2 1

Distributed by Pomegranate Europe Ltd.
Unit 1, Heathcote Business Centre, Hurlbutt Road
Warwick, Warwickshire CV34 6TD, UK
[+44] 0 1926 430111
sales@pomeurope.co.uk

This product is in compliance with the Consumer Product Safety Improvement Act of 2008 (CPSIA). A General Conformity Certificate concerning Pomegranate's compliance with the CPSIA is available on our website at www.pomegranate.com, or by request at 800 227 1428.
For additional CPSIA-required tracking details, contact Pomegranate at 800 227 1428.

1. Penny Candy

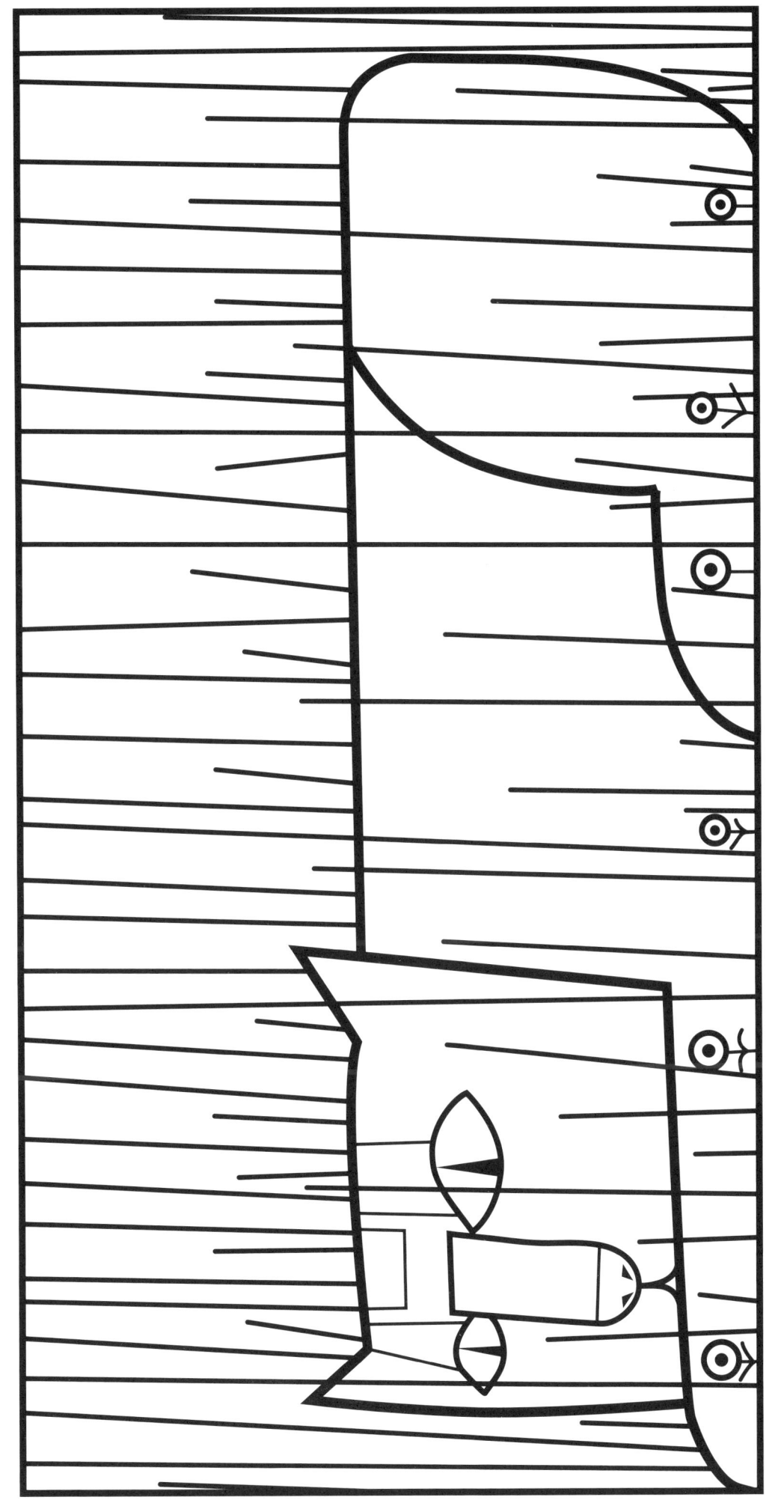

2. Spring Creeper

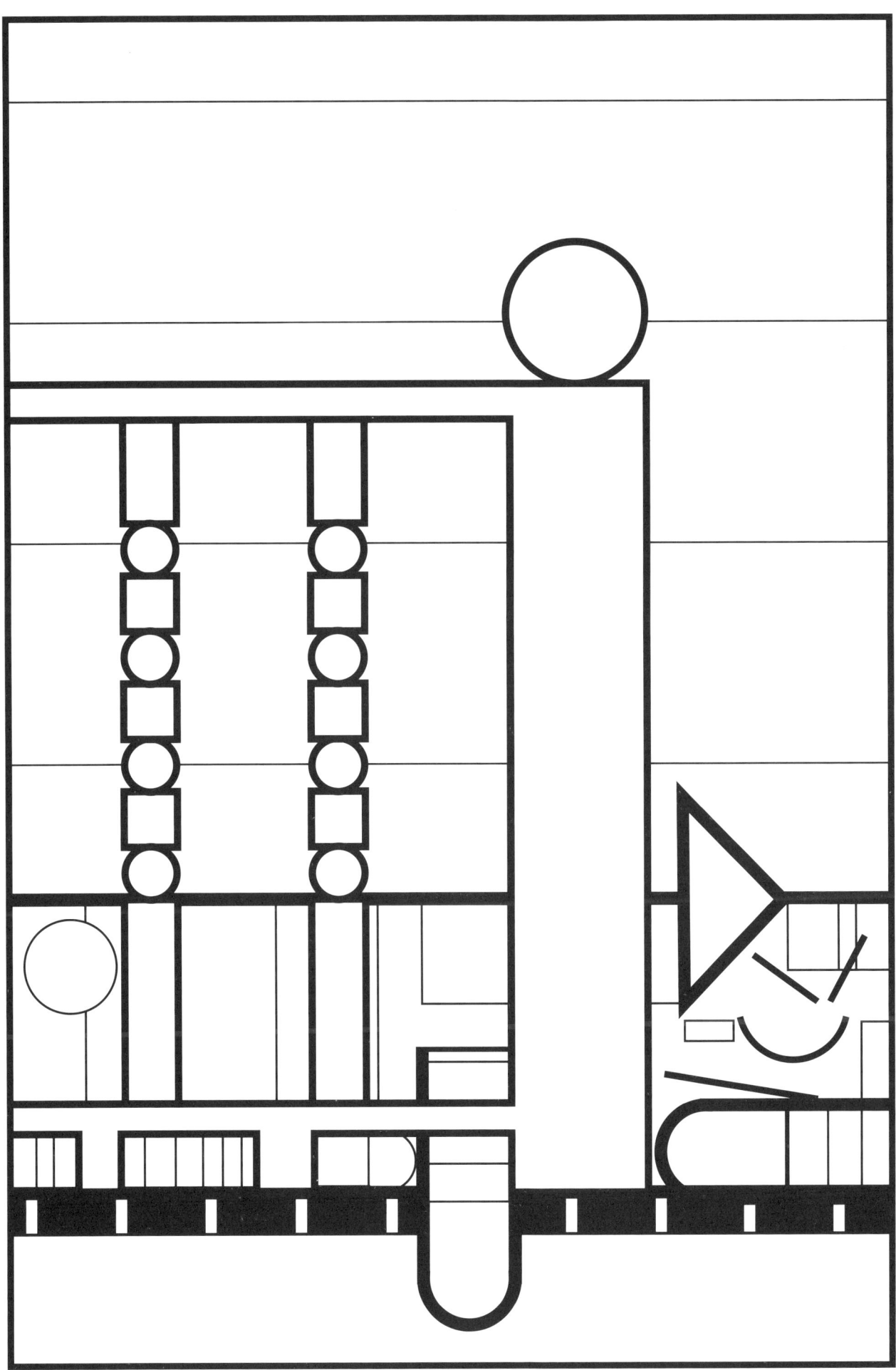

3. Summer Watch

4. Crazy Cat, Crazy Quilt

5. Noazark

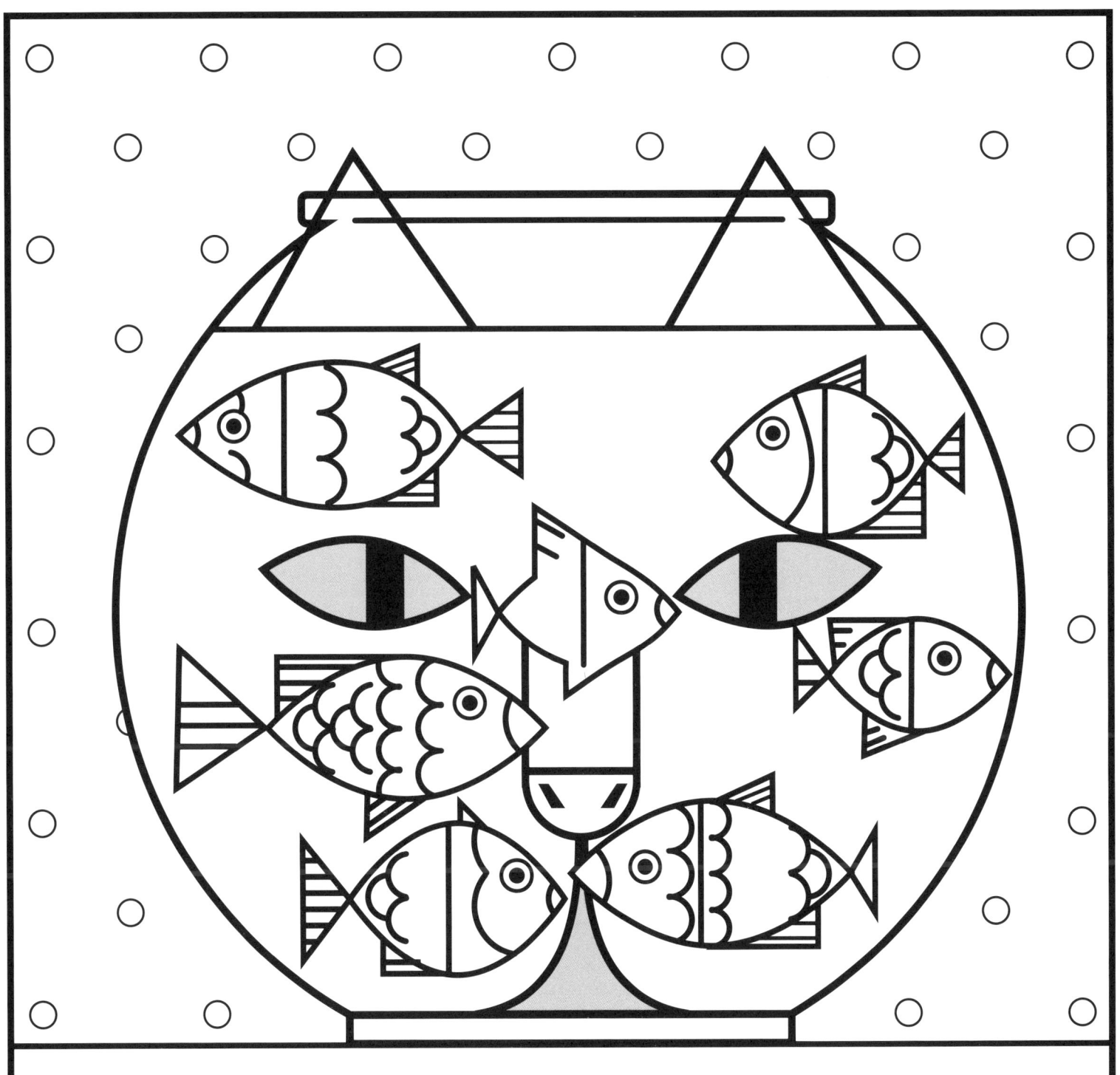

6. Fishful Thinking

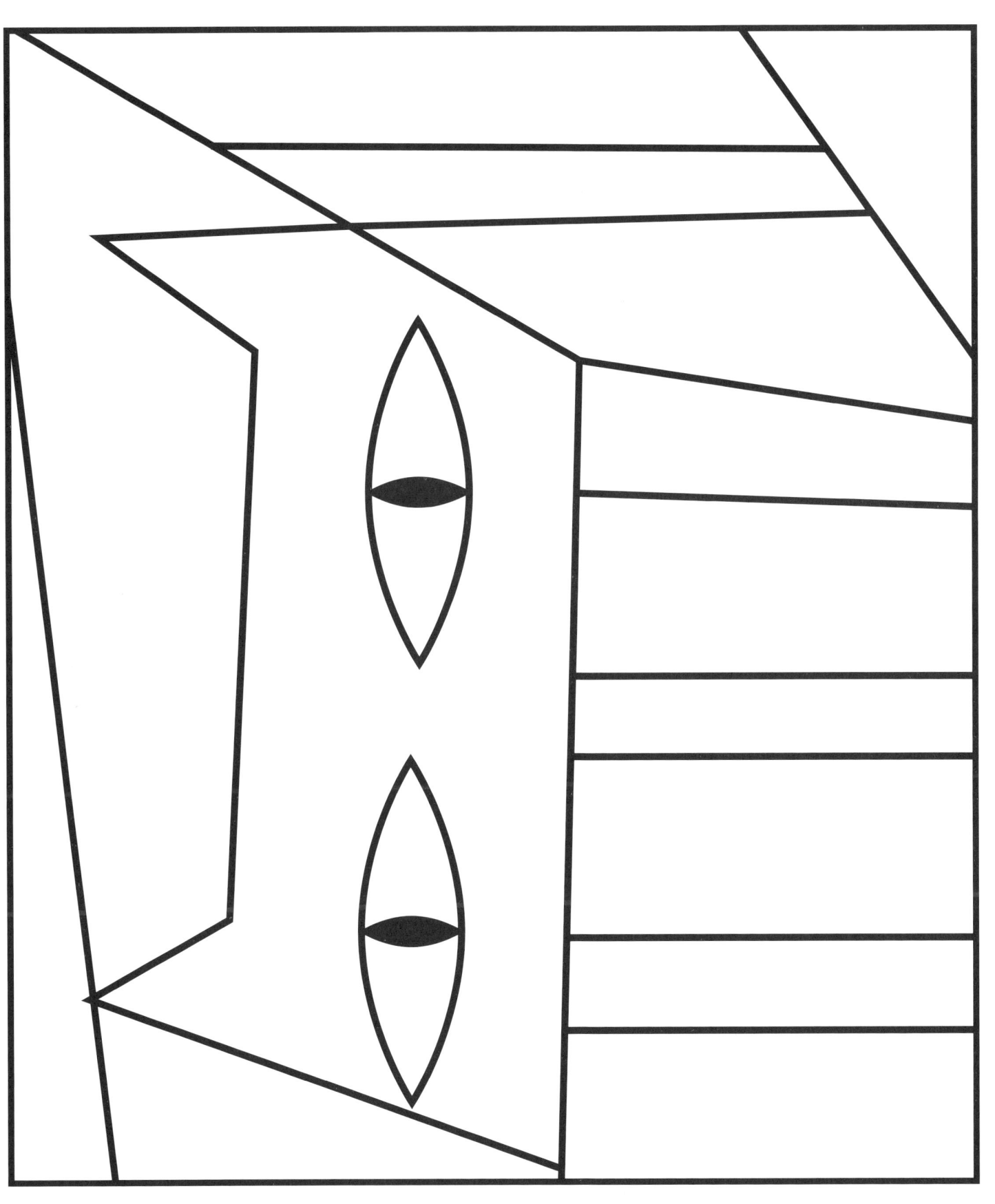
7. Cat in a Hatbox

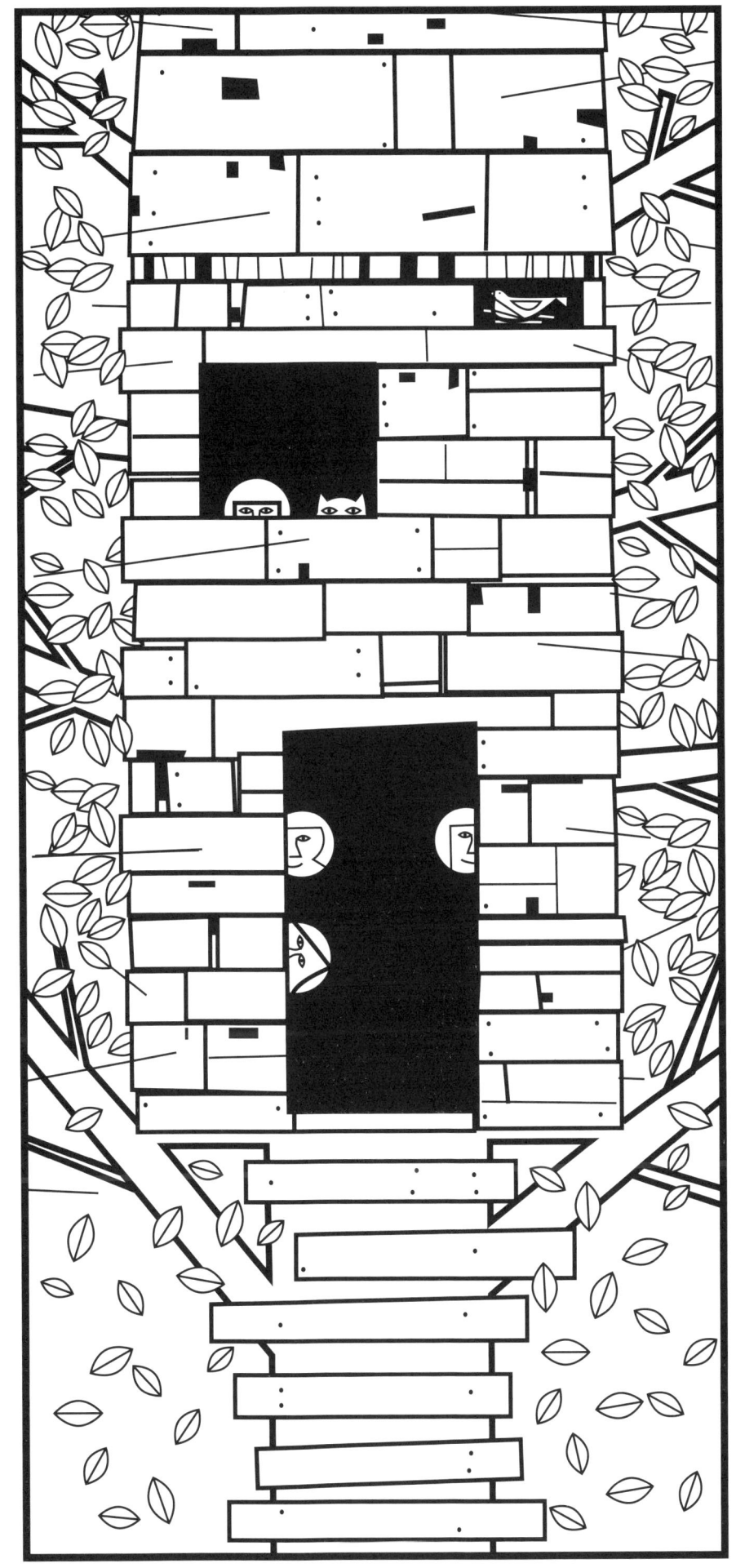

8. Treehouse

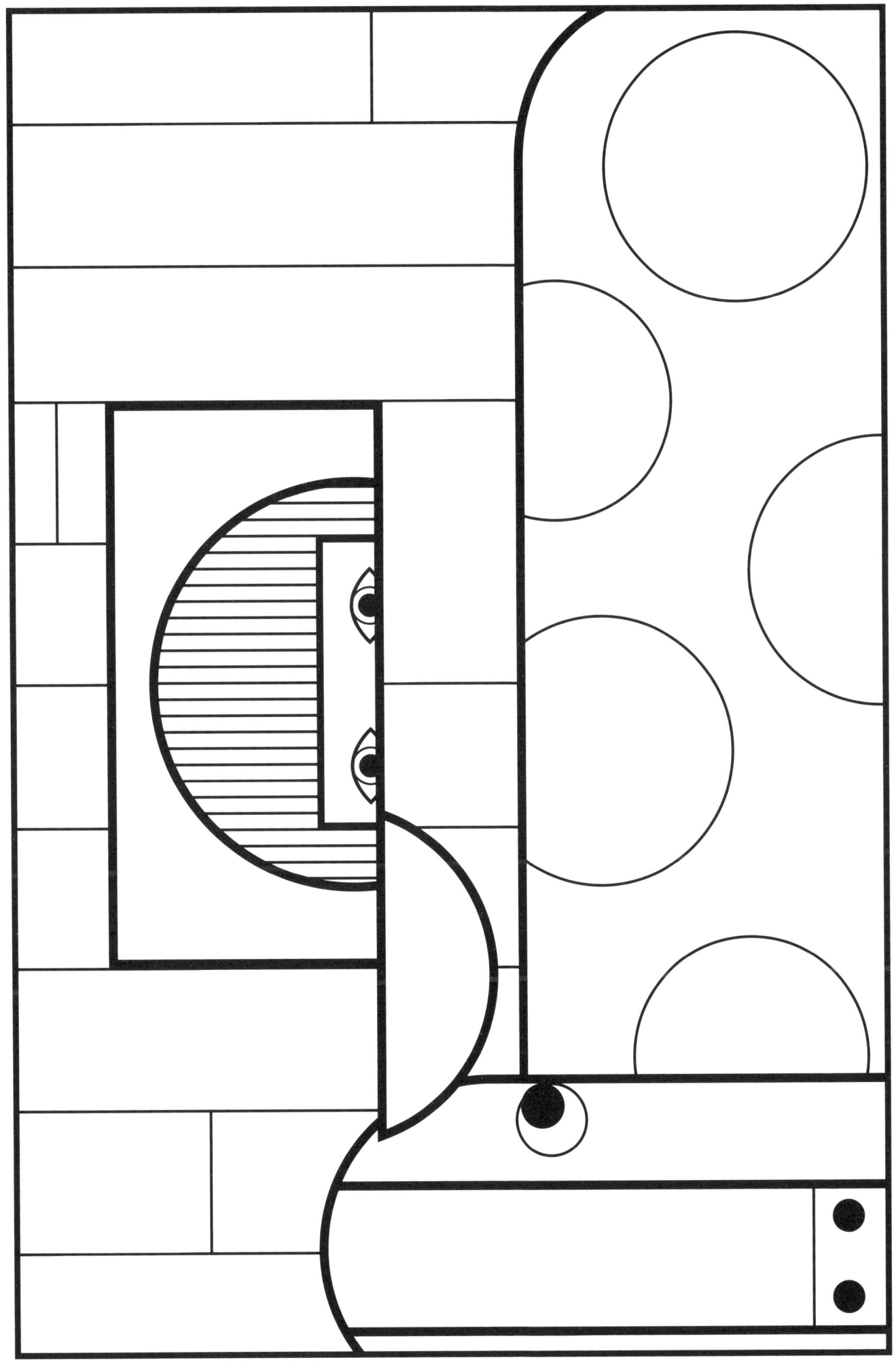

9. Milking Megan the Moo Cow

10. Baskit

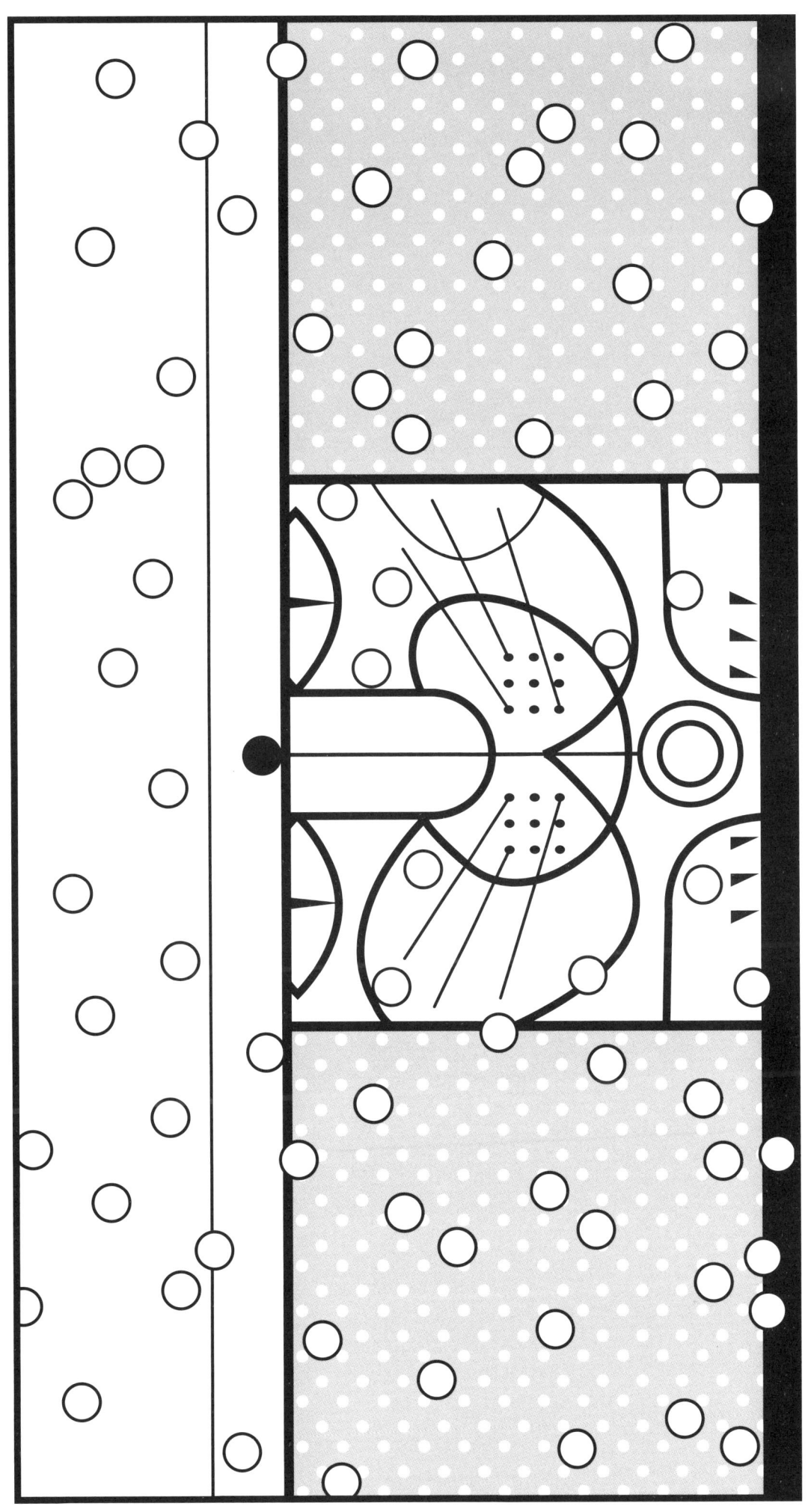

11. Winter Watch

12. Specially for You

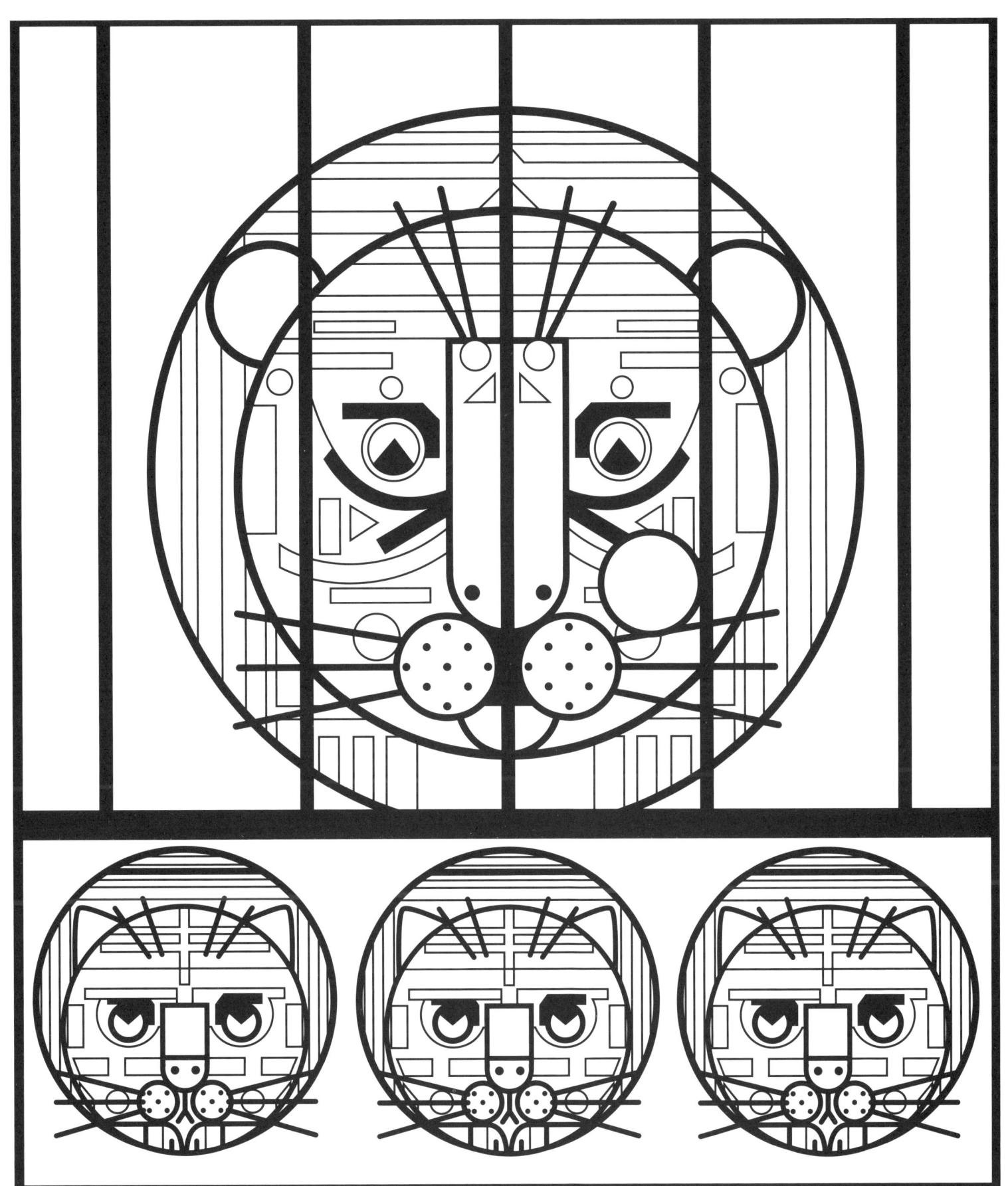

13. Copy Cats

14. Orange Cat

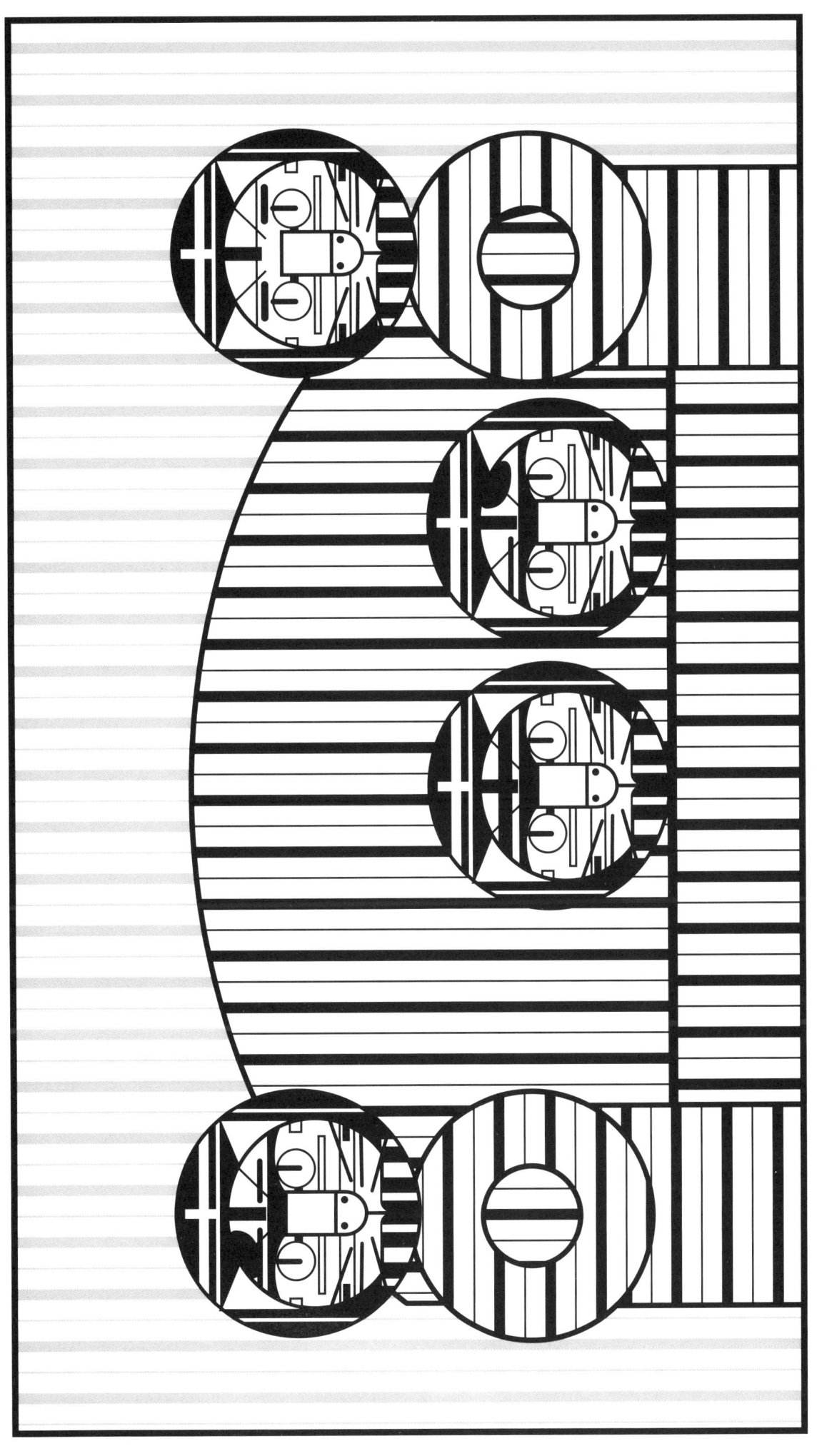

15. Couch Petatoes

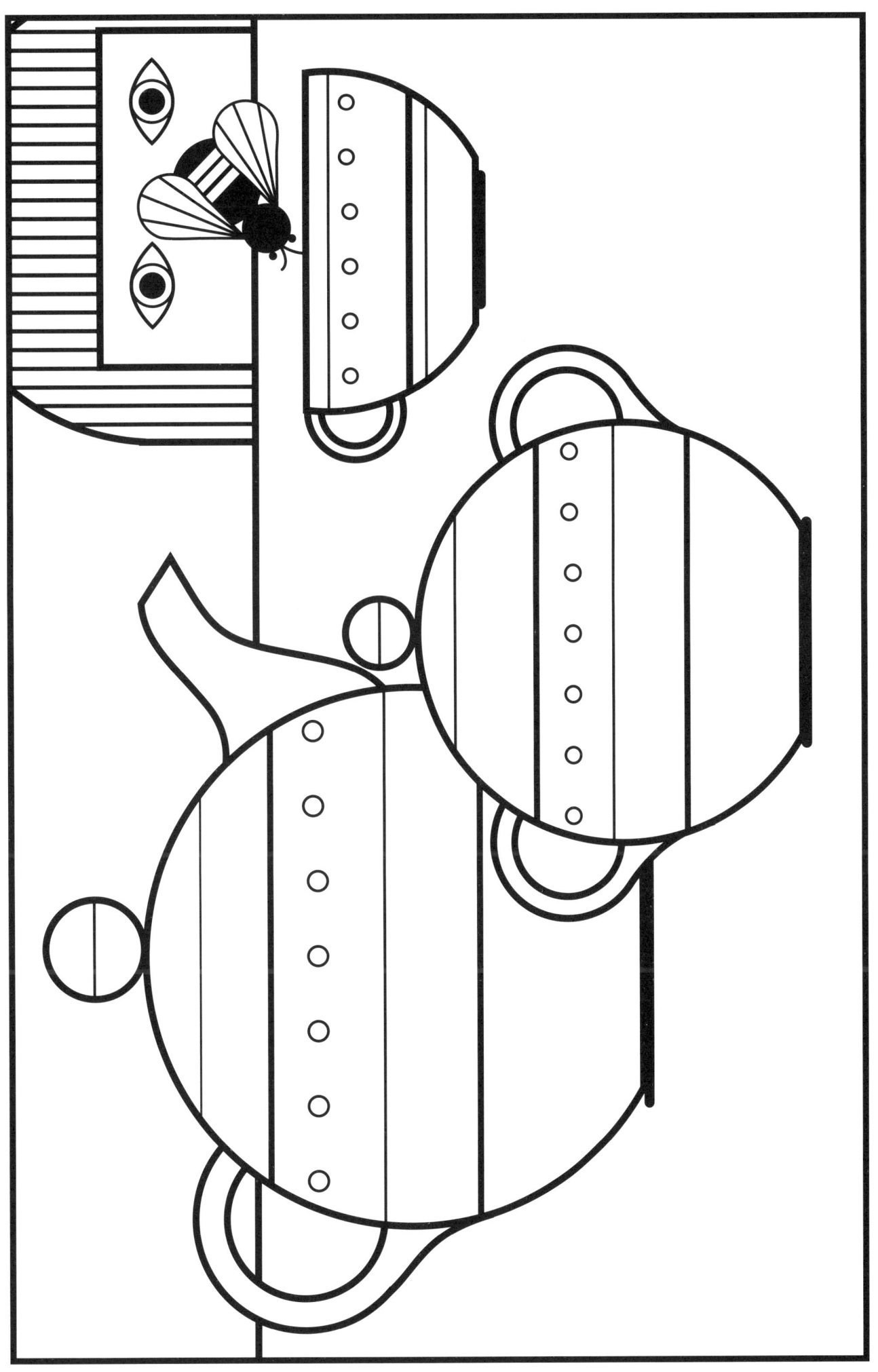

16. Tea with Penelope the Bee

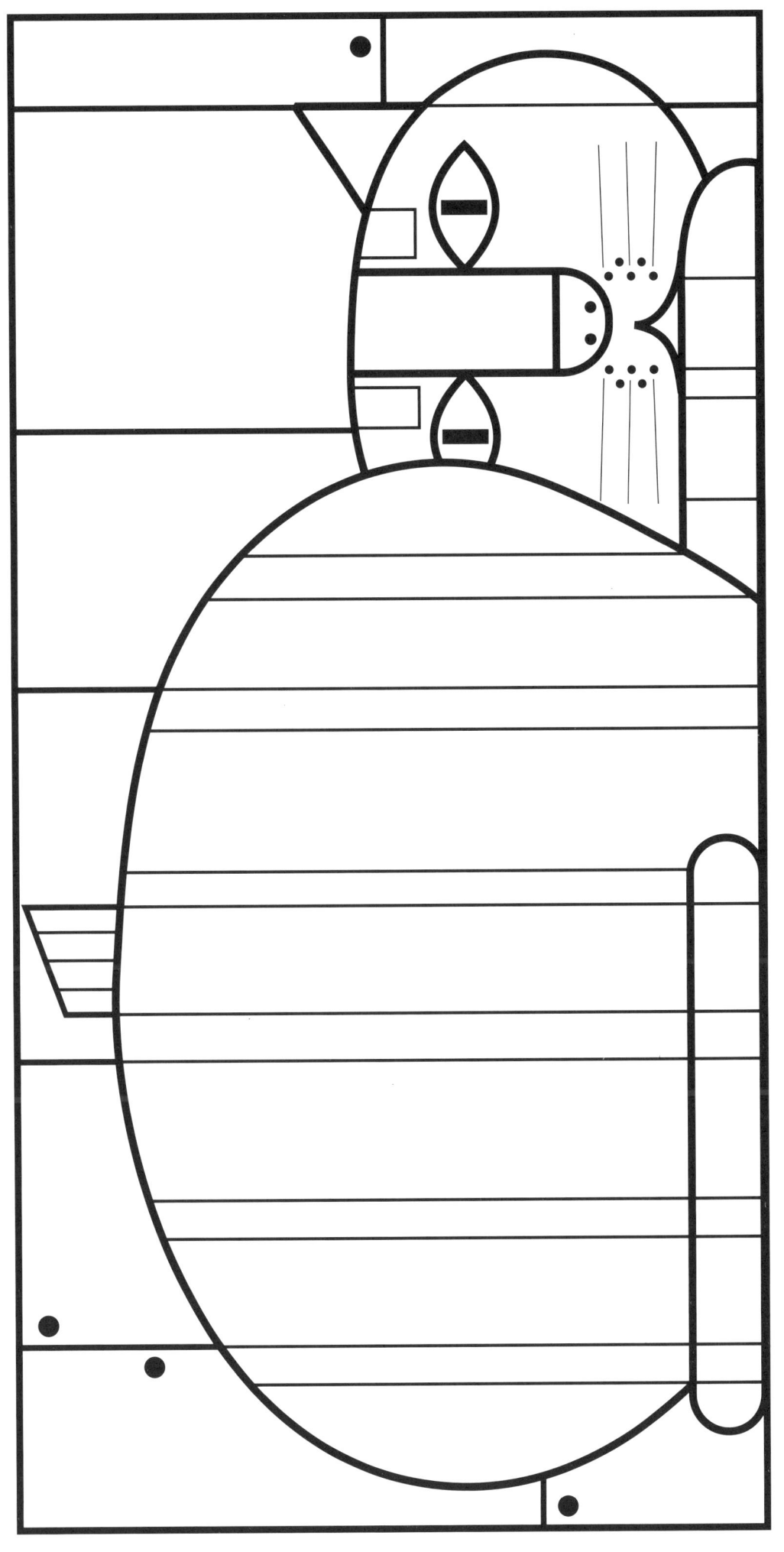

17. Peepkin

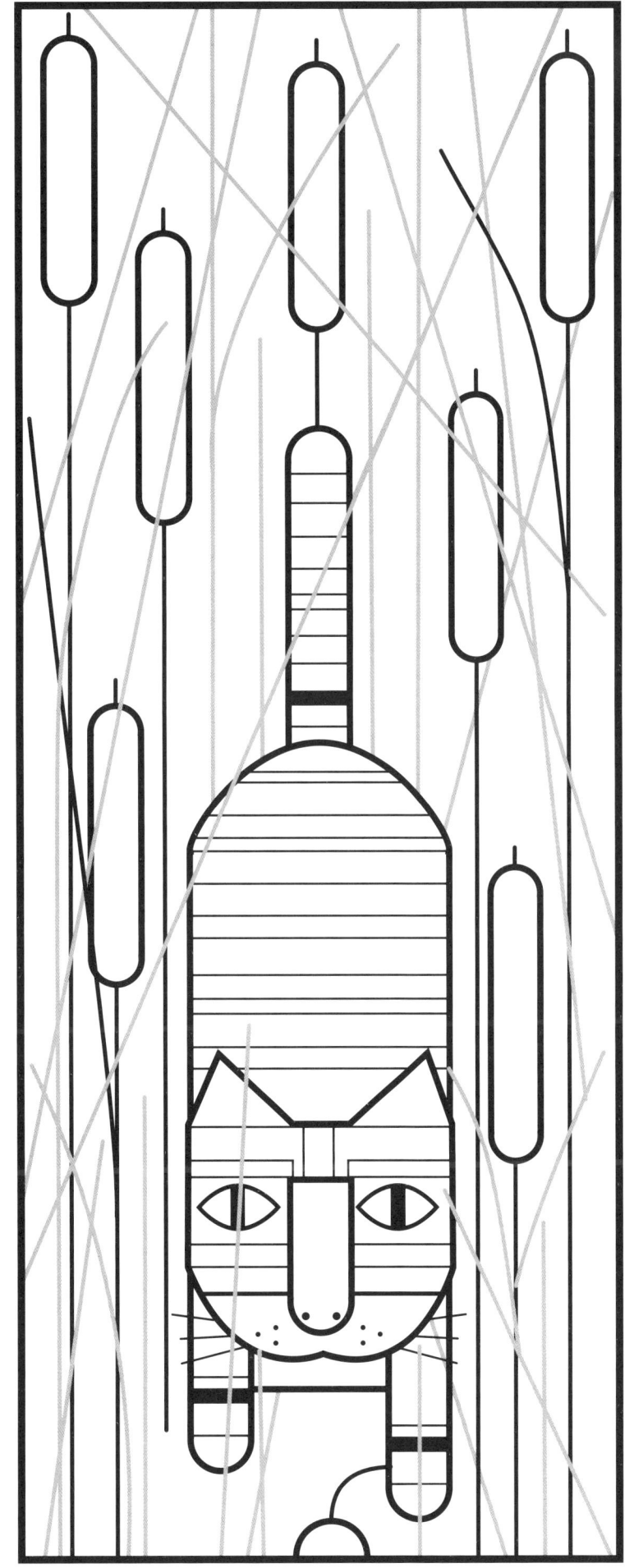

18. Nine Tails

19. Kitten 'n Knittin'

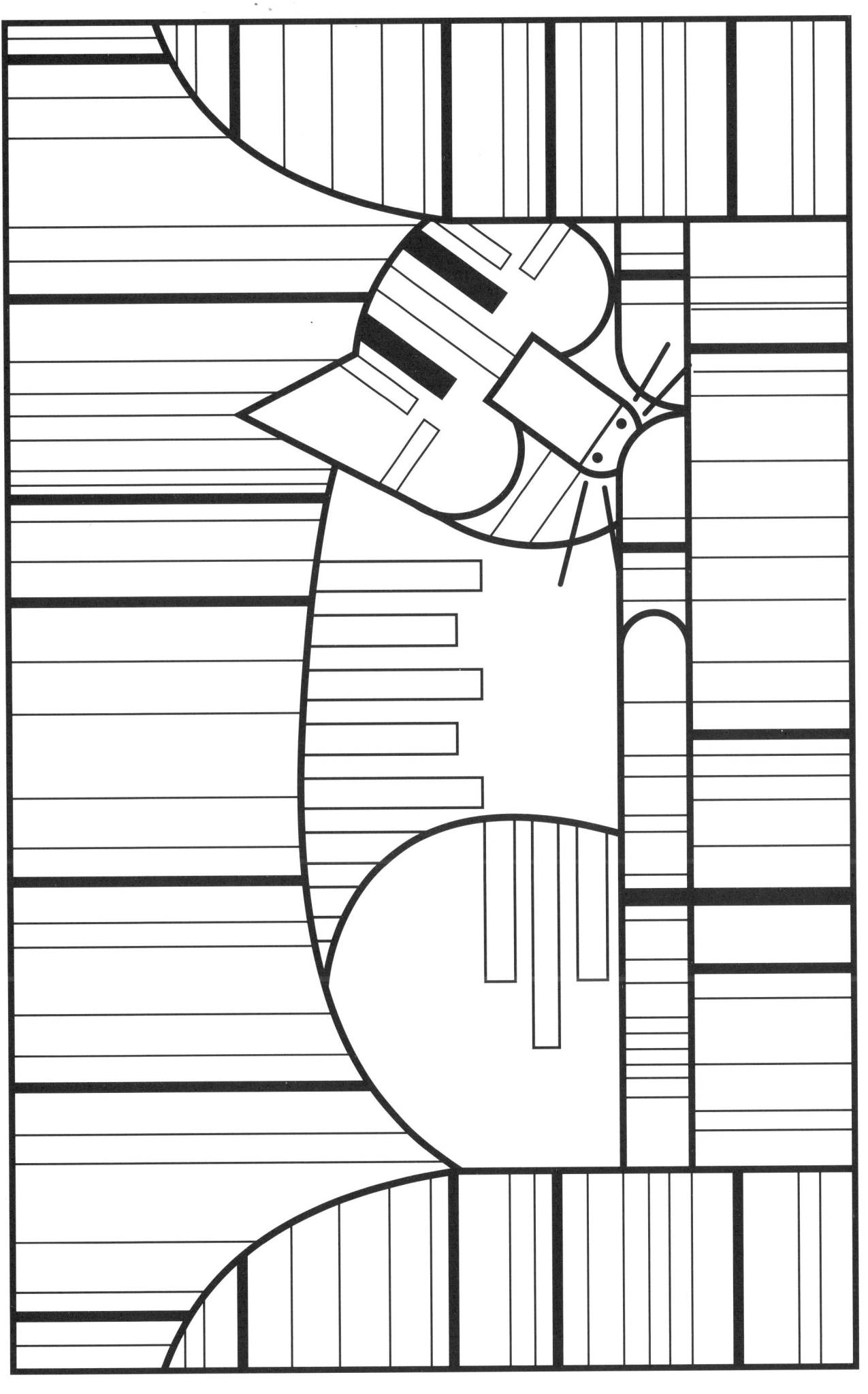
20. Sleepy Time Tom

Draw and color your own picture here!

Draw and color your own picture here!

Draw and color your own picture here!